D0495752

THE
BRO
CODE

THE
BRO
CODE

BARNEY STINSON
with MATT KUHN

**SIMON &
SCHUSTER**

London · New York · Sydney · Toronto · New Delhi

A CBS COMPANY

First published in Great Britain by Simon & Schuster UK Ltd, 2009
A CBS COMPANY

™ & © by Twentieth Century Fox Film Corporation, 2008

This book is copyright under the Berne Convention.
No reproduction without permission.
All rights reserved.

The right of Matt Kuhn to be identified as the author of this
work has been asserted by him in accordance with sections 77 and 78
of the Copyright, Designs and Patents Act, 1988.

28

Simon & Schuster UK Ltd
1st Floor
222 Gray's Inn Road
London
WC1X 8HB

www.simonandschuster.co.uk

Simon & Schuster Australia, Sydney
Simon & Schuster India, New Delhi

A CIP catalogue for this book is available
from the British Library.

ISBN: 978-1-84739-930-4

iPhone and iPod touch are trademarks of Apple Inc.

Designed by Timothy Shaner, nightanddaydesign.biz
Illustrations by Jennifer Hendriks

Printed and bound by CPI Group (UK) Ltd, Croydon, CR0 4YY

For me,
the best Bro I know

TABLE OF CONTENTS

INTRODUCTION

Whether we know it or not, each of us lives a life governed by an internalized code of conduct. Some call it morality. Others call it religion. I call it "the Bro Code."

For centuries men have attempted to follow this code with no universal understanding of what such an arrangement meant: Is it okay to hug a Bro?* If I'm invited to a Bro's wedding, do I really have to bring a gift?† Can I sleep with a Bro's sister or mother or both?‡

Now, for the first time on paper, I have recorded the rules of social decorum that Bros have practiced since the dawn of man . . . if not before. The Bro Code previously existed only as an oral tradition (heh), so I have journeyed the globe to piece

---

* Never.
† Nope.
‡ Dude. Come on.

together and transcribe the scattered fragments of the Bro Code, pausing only to flesh it out myself (double heh). While not intending to write a "Guide to Being a Bro," if men should treat it as such and pass this compendium of knowledge from one generation to the next, I have little doubt it would bring a tear to my eye. But *not* out of it. That would be a violation of Article 41: A Bro never cries.

It is my hope that, with a better understanding of the Bro Code, Bros the world over can put aside their differences and strengthen the bonds of brotherhood. It is then, and only then, that we might work together as one to accomplish perhaps the most important challenge society faces—getting laid. Before dismissing this pursuit as crass and ignoble, consider this postulate: without the sport inherent in trying to bang chicks, would men willingly have sex for the sole purpose of producing smelly, screaming babies?*

* Of course not

Centuries from now, when a Bro applies the rudiments of the Bro Code to score a three-boobed future chick, the only thanks I'll need is the knowledge that I—in whatever small capacity—Bro'd him out . . . though if he could figure out how to bring me back to life, that would be pretty awesome, too.

—Barney Stinson

WHAT IS A BRO?

You've probably heard the word "Bro" used liberally at your local bar or gym. Perhaps you've seen it recklessly confused with "dude" or "guy" in an adventure-themed soft-drink commercial. Maybe even you yourself have unwittingly tossed out a "Bro" when asking a stranger for the time. But an important distinction must be drawn: just because a guy is a dude, doesn't mean that dude is a Bro.

Q: *What is a Bro?*

A: A Bro is a person who would give you the shirt off his back when he doesn't want to wear it anymore. A Bro is a person who will bend over backwards to help you bend someone else over backwards. In short, a Bro is a lifelong companion you can trust will always be there for you, unless he's got something else going on.

Q: Who is your Bro?

A: Your mailman is a Bro, your father was once a Bro, and the boy who mows your lawn represents the Bro of tomorrow, but that doesn't make him *your* Bro. When someone has faithfully upheld one or more of the codes in the Bro Code, then you may consider him your Bro. *Warning:* Exercise caution when bringing home a hot chick—your brother may or may not be your Bro.

Q: Can only dudes be Bros?

A: You don't need to be a guy to be somebody's Bro, provided you uphold the moral values contained within this sacred canon. When a woman sets a guy up with her busty friend, she's acting as a Bro. And if she sets him up with other hot friends after he slept with the first one and never called her again, then she's officially his Bro.

BROCABULARY

As you thumb through *The Bro Code*, you may come across some words and terms you've never seen before. Many have been boldfaced and placed in the Glossary on page 193 so you can familiarize yourself with the **Bronacular.**

While Bros are always encouraged to spread the truth of the Bro Code, they are also cautioned against overusing "Bro." Such **Broliferation** cheapens the important mission of this book and, nearly as important, makes you sound stupid.

APPROPRIATE "BRO" USAGE	INAPPROPRIATE "BRO" USAGE
Nabroleon	*Broan of Arc*
Tom Brokaw	*Brobara Walters*
Bro Jackson	*Bro J. Simpson*
Teddy Broosevelt	*Geraldine Ferrarbro*
Broce Springsteen	*Broko Ono*

ORIGIN

While the story of the Bro Code is not nearly as simple and elegant as God handing down some stone tablets to Broses, its origins weave all the way back to the dawn of humanity.

In the beginning there was no Bro Code . . . which was unfortunate for the world's first Bros—Cain and Abel. Lacking an agreed-upon set of social principles, Cain killed Abel and committed history's first **Broicide**. As punishment Cain was doomed to walk the earth alone. Why? Because without a wingman, he had absolutely no chance to meet chicks.

Centuries later a Bro from Sparta and a Bro from Troy got in a fight over a chick named Helen. I know, "Helen" doesn't sound hot, but allegedly she had a "face that launched a thousand ships," so you can just imagine what her rack was like. The two Bros waged a terrible war over this chick—a war that could have been avoided had the Bros been familiar with the most basic Bro Code: Bros before ho's. Troy put up a good fight, but the Spartan navy was very powerful. Soon hordes of Spartan seamen burst through the Trojan barrier, and Helen got half the gold for the next eighteen years.

Hundreds of years later, appropriately in Philadelphia (the City of Bro Love), a little known delegate named Barnabas Stinson scratched on parchment what is now considered the earliest attempt to record the Bro Code. Over the years Bros have amended and added rules, but Stinson's elegant words remain as the glorious preamble to the Bro Code.

While the original document is housed two stories beneath sea level in an undisclosed, vacuum-sealed, bullet-proof chamber, I was able to gain access long enough to manufacture this replica.

The Bro Code

When in the course of human events it becomes necessary for Bros to settle a dispute, decent respect to the opinions of Bro= kind requires that they should declare the causes which impel them to argue, though prudence says it's probably a chick. We hold these truths to be self=evident, that all Bros are created equal—though not necessarily with the same good looks or sense of style—and that they are endowed with certain inalienable rights, that among these are life, liberty, and the pursuit of tail. To secure these rights, we present the Bro Code. It is the right of Bros to alter or to abolish it, and to institute a new code, but let's face it—that's a lot of work.

Be it here resolved that, henceforth, when and if two gentlemen covet the company of the same wench, the Bro who first calleth dibs on said wench shall be entitled sufferance for such time as it takes to reasonably strike out, or the time it takes sand to fill one half of an hourglass, whichever comes first. At no point is it permissible for a Bro to violate this right and codpiece block his Bro, even if he hath consumed copious quantities of ale.

THE
BRO
CODE

☞ ARTICLE 1 ☜

Bros before ho's.

The bond between two men is stronger than the bond between a man and a woman because, on average, men are stronger than women. That's just science

---

DID YOU KNOW . . .
Article 1 can trace *its* genesis all the way back to Genesis. No, not the Peter Gabriel/Phil Collins pop triad, but the biblical book. The discovery of the Dead Sea Scrolls has unearthed a once-lost passage that documents the earliest infringement of the Bro Code.

BOOK OF BARNABAS 1:1

And everything of need was provided in the Garden. Fruit, water, companionship. But one day, Adam came upon a naked chick, Eve, and desired her olive leaf. And so Adam wenteth behind an apple tree to know Eve, totally ditching his Bro, Phil, who had Knicks tickets. Courtside. Long story short, humankind became self-aware, paradise was lost, and well, we all know what happened to the Knicks.

☞ ARTICLE 2 ☜

A Bro is always entitled to do something stupid, as long as the rest of his Bros are all doing it.

NOTE: Had Butch Cassidy come charging out of that cabin alone, people would have been like, "Dude, come on." If only one Spanish dude had decided to run down the street in front of a bunch of angry bulls, people would've been like, "Dude, come on." If only Tommy Lee had worn eyeliner in the early days of Mötley Crüe, people would have been like, "Lady, come on." The license to be stupid is why we have Bros in the first place.

☞ ARTICLE 3 ☜

If a Bro gets a dog, it must be at least as tall as his knee when full-grown.

COROLLARY: Naming a lapdog after a pro wrestler or a character from a Steve McQueen movie does not absolve a Bro from the spirit of this article.

⌒ ARTICLE 4 ⌒

A Bro never divulges the existence of the Bro Code to a woman. It is a sacred document not to be shared with chicks for any reason . . . no, not even that reason.

NOTE: If you are a woman reading this, first, let me apologize: it was never my intention for this book to contain so much math.

Second, I urge you to look at this document for what it is—a piece of fiction meant to entertain a broad audience through the prism of stereotypical gender differences. I mean, sometimes it really *is* like we're from different planets! Clearly, no real person would actually believe or adhere to the vulgar rules contained within.* Those boots are adorable, b-t-dub.

---

* Psst—hey, guys! I put this in really small type at the bottom since we all know men have much better vision than women. Ignore the above—the Bro Code is definitely *not* a piece of fiction. I was simply lying to uphold this very article.

⌐ ARTICLE 5 ⌐

*Whether he cares about sports
or not, a Bro cares about sports.*

~ ARTICLE 6 ~

A Bro shall not lollygag if he must get naked in front of other Bros in a gym locker room.

COROLLARY: If a Bro gets naked in the locker room, all other Bros shall pretend that nothing out of the ordinary is happening while, at the same time, immediately averting their eyes. When in doubt, remember the old adage: "If a towel drops to the floor, so should your eyes."

⌒ ARTICLE 7 ⌒

A Bro never admits he can't drive stick. Even after an accident.

☞ ARTICLE 8 ☜

A Bro never sends a greeting card to another Bro.

There are no sentiments between Bros that cannot be articulated through the convenience and emotional distance of electronic mail. The following are a few emails for any **Brocassion** that succinctly get the message across without costing you the trouble and expense of having to find and then send an actual greeting card.

EMAILS FOR ANY BROCCASION

SYMPATHY

To:	Bro
From:	Bro
Subject:	Dude

Sorry, Bro.

CONGRATULATIONS

To:	Bro
From:	Bro
Subject:	Bro!

Nice, Bro!

GET WELL SOON

To:	Bro
From:	Bro
Subject:	Bro. . .

Don't give up, Bro.

HAPPY BIRTHDAY

To:	Bro
From:	Bro
Subject:	Dude

Drinks on me, Bro.

THINKING OF YOU

To:	N/A
From:	N/A
Subject:	N/A

N/A

☞ ARTICLE 9 ☜

Should a Bro lose a body part due to an accident or illness, his fellow Bros will not make lame jokes such as "Gimme three!" or "Wow, quitting your job like that really took a lot of ball." It's still a high five and that Bro still has a lot of balls . . . metaphorically speaking, of course.

⌐ ARTICLE 10 ⌐

A Bro will drop whatever he's doing and rush to help his Bro dump a chick.

It's normal for a Bro to get confused and disoriented when dumping a chick. For some reason he's worried she'll become agitated or even violent after he calmly explains his desire to have sex with her friends. This is when a Bro most needs his Bro to remind him that there are plenty of chicks in the ocean, and that a breakup need not be hazardous, stressful, or even time-consuming.

SIDE-BRO: HOW TO DUMP A CHICK IN SIX WORDS OR LESS

"Maybe try a side salad instead."
"Cute! You're growing a mustache, too!"
"She looks like a younger you."
"I will finance a boob job."
"Sorry I threw out your shoes."
"Your sister let me do that."

☞ ARTICLE 11 ☜

A Bro may ask his Bro(s) to help him move, but only after first disclosing an honest estimate on both time commitment and number of large pieces of furniture. If the Bro has vastly underestimated either, his Bros retain the right to leave his possessions where they are—in most cases, stuck in a doorway.

⌒ ARTICLE 12 ⌒

Bros do not share dessert.

⌒ ARTICLE 13 ⌒

All Bros shall dub one of their Bros his wingman.

MIX AND MATCH: FAMOUS WINGMEN

Michael Jordan ❏   ❏ Scooby

Snoopy ❏   ❏ Dan Quayle

Han Solo ❏   ❏ Hot Wings

George H. W. Bush ❏   ❏ Woodstock

Bert ❏   ❏ Chewbacca

Shaggy ❏   ❏ Scottie Pippen

Beer ❏   ❏ Ernie

⌐ ARTICLE 14 ⌐

*If a chick inquires about another Bro's sexual history, a Bro shall honor the **Brode of Silence** and play dumb. Better to have women think all men are stupid than to tell the truth.*

⇁ ARTICLE 15 ↽

A Bro never dances with his hands above his head.

ARTICLE 16

A Bro should be able, at any time, to recite the following reigning champions: Super Bowl, World Series, and Playmate of the Year.

A Bro shall be kind and courteous to his co-workers, unless they are beneath him on the Pyramid of Screaming.

America was built on the backs of men and women who were yelled at to work harder, and the tradition has been screamed from generation to generation. But you can't just scream at anybody . . . you can only scream at those beneath you. To illustrate how it works, here's the Scream Pyramid for a professional football team:

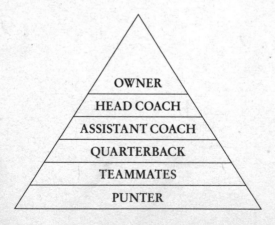

OWNER
HEAD COACH
ASSISTANT COACH
QUARTERBACK
TEAMMATES
PUNTER

It's no different inside the office, as exemplified by my own corporate Scream Pyramid:

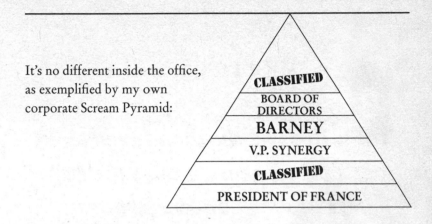

CLASSIFIED
BOARD OF DIRECTORS
BARNEY
V.P. SYNERGY
CLASSIFIED
PRESIDENT OF FRANCE

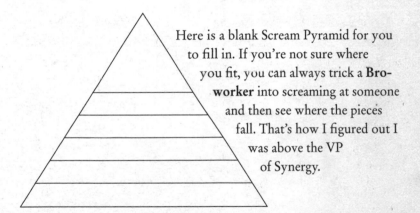

Here is a blank Scream Pyramid for you to fill in. If you're not sure where you fit, you can always trick a **Bro-worker** into screaming at someone and then see where the pieces fall. That's how I figured out I was above the VP of Synergy.

IMPORTANT NOTE: If you find yourself at the bottom, don't fret. The beauty of the pyramid is that you can always add a layer to the foundation. The janitorial crew, the sleepy-eyed security man, or anyone who doesn't speak English is a great place to start.

⤳ ARTICLE 18 ⤳

If a Bro spearheads a beer run at a party, he is entitled to any excess monies accrued after canvassing the group.

NOTE: To avoid confrontation, it's a good idea for the Bro to jettison the receipt before returning to the party.

☞ ARTICLE 19 ☜

A Bro shall not sleep with another Bro's sister. However, a Bro shall not get angry if another Bro says, "Dude, your sister's hot!"

COROLLARY: It's probably best for everyone if Bros just hide pictures of their sisters when other Bros are coming over.

CHECKLIST FOR **BRO-PROOFING** YOUR HOME

- ❏ Hide all pictures of hot sisters, moms, and first cousins.
- ❏ Open liquor bottles and dust the bar area to give the impression you actually use it.
- ❏ As a courtesy, move printed porn from the bedroom to the bathroom.
- ❏ Scan DVR playlist and remove embarrassing television programs like daytime talk shows.
- ❏ Open all windows.
- ❏ Display all remote controls on the coffee table, regardless of functionality.
- ❏ Disconnect answering machine, or . . .
- ❏ Call Mom an hour before your Bros arrive.
- ❏ Coasters, coasters, coasters!
- ❏ Sign out of email account.
- ❏ Usher girlfriend/booty call off the premises.

ᗡ ARTICLE 20 ᗡ

A Bro respects his Bros in the military because they've selflessly chosen to defend the nation, but more to the point, because they can kick his ass six ways to Sunday.

⇗ ARTICLE 21 ⇖

A Bro never shares observations about another Bro's smoking-hot girlfriend. Even if the Bro with the hot girlfriend attempts to bait the Bro by saying, "She's smoking-hot, huh?" a Bro shall remain silent, because in this situation, he's the only one who should be baiting.

⌒ ARTICLE 22 ⌒

There is no law that prohibits a woman from being a Bro.

W omen make excellent Bros. Why? Because they can translate and navigate the confusing and contradictory whims that comprise the Chick Code.

DO CHICKS REALLY HAVE THEIR OWN CODE?

Yes, I'm afraid so. One morning, just before slipping out the door while my hostess was in the shower, I happened upon a copy of the rumored tome. I didn't have time to flip much past the pink bedazzled cover, but here are some of the phrases I remember seeing on the frilly pages within:

- A chick shall not sleep with another chick's ex-boyfriend, unless she does.

- A chick never pays for anything. Ever.

- If two chicks get into a fight, they shall make catty remarks and pretend to ignore each other, rather than simply stripping down and wrestling it out.

- If a chick hears a chick-empowerment song like "I Will Survive," she shall stop whatever she's doing, grab another chick's hand, and shriek the lyrics at the top of her lungs.

- A chick may get a dog as a pet, but only if it fits in her mailbox.

- If two chicks are wearing the same outfit, each retains the right to accidentally spill a drink on the other.

- A chick shall not operate a motor vehicle in a safe manner.

- A chick has a free pass to slut it up on Halloween.

⌁ ARTICLE 23 ⌁

When flipping through TV channels with his Bros, a Bro is not allowed to skip past a program featuring boobs. This includes, but is not limited to, exercise shows, women's athletics, and on some occasions, surgery programs.

~ ARTICLE 24 ~

When wearing a baseball cap, a Bro may position the brim at either 12 or 6 o'clock. All other angles are reserved for rappers and the handicapped.

⌐ ARTICLE 25 ⌐

A Bro doesn't let another Bro get a tattoo, particularly a tattoo of a girl's name.

The average relationship between a man and a woman lasts eighty-three days. The relationship between a man and his skin lasts a lifetime and must be nurtured, because as we all know, the skin is the largest and second most important organ a man has.

BARNEY STINSON'S FIELD GUIDE TO TATTOOS

TATTOO	TRANSLATION
	*"Hey, everybody, look at me! Not only have I made the foolish mistake of choosing a lifetime of monogamy, but I have permanently branded myself as off-limits."*

TATTOO	TRANSLATION
	*"Hey, everybody, look at me! This band looks like a scar of manhood that I earned after my village banished me to the hinterlands for seven days with no food or water . . . like in that Kevin Bacon basketball movie."*
	*"Hey, everybody, look at me! I have a fearsome dragon on my arm! Are you scared? Good, because I'm hoping this baby wards off intruders from my mom's basement."*

TATTOO	TRANSLATION
	*"Hey, everybody, look at me! I'm governed by an Eastern philosophy, as these significant Cantonese and/or Mandarin characters chiseled into my flesh may or may not indicate. If I spoke or read this particular language, perhaps I could explain my perspective more clearly, but I guess you'll just have to take the scary-looking tattoo artist's word for it. I know I did."*
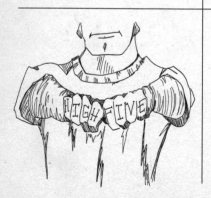	*"Hey, everybody, look at me! There's an important message inked on my fingers. It has to be ten letters or less and you can only read it when I'm waterskiing or getting arrested, but still, it's an important message that wholly represents my creed."*

☞ ARTICLE 26 ☜

Unless he has children, a Bro shall not wear his cell phone on a belt clip.

⌐ ARTICLE 27 ⌐

A Bro never removes his shirt in front of other Bros, unless at a resort pool or the beach.

COROLLARY: A Bro with a coat of fur on his back keeps that thing covered at all times, even at a resort pool or the beach. Sorry, Bro.

⌒ ARTICLE 28 ⌒

A Bro will, in a timely manner, alert his Bro to the existence of a girl fight.

A Bro must, in a timely manner, communicate the possibility of fisticuffs between two humans of the female variety (Henceforth "**girl fight**"), in an effort to make possible and probable that another Bro or Bros can partake in observation. A "timely manner" is open to interpretation based on the initial Bro's viewing and processing of the potential feminine conflagration. Said Bro must use any and all methods of media distribution at his disposal, including but not limited to: telecommunications, elbow nudging, carrier pigeons, fiber optics, shouting, postcards, and telepathy. If an informed Bro is unable to witness the girl fight firsthand, the spotter Bro is responsible for documenting and relating details of the girl fight via pictures, video, or, barring any other reasonable method, interpretive dance and/or pantomime.

If two Bros decide to catch a movie together, they may not attend a screening that begins after 4:40 PM. Also, despite the cost savings, they shall not split a tub of popcorn, choosing instead to procure individual bags.

⁀ ARTICLE 30 ⁀

A Bro doesn't comparison shop.

ARTICLE 31

When on the prowl, a Bro hits on the hottest chick first because you just never know.

CURRENT HOT CHICK RATINGS

1. Half-Asian Chicks	↑2	Multiethnic? Multi*yes*nic!
2. Lebanese Girls	↓1	Leba*please* girls!
3. Politician's Daughters	↓1	Daddy's issues ≠ Daddy's issues
4. Mute Women	↔	One thing's for sure: they are handy
5. Eighties Music Video Chicks	↑112	Crawled over a Corvette hood into the top ten

6. Really Tall Chicks	↑4	Can reach the ceiling fan . . . from the bed
7. Mermaids	↔	Wet. Wild. Wonderful.
8. Chicks Raised in a Cult	↑883	Guaranteed crazy factor
9. Army Chicks	↓4	Drop and give us something . . . please!
10. Girls on Rollerblades	↓4	Too fast, too furious

☞ ARTICLE 32 ☜

A Bro doesn't allow another Bro to get married until he's at least thirty.

~ ARTICLE 33 ~

When in a public restroom, a Bro (1) stares straight ahead when using the urinal; (2) makes the obligatory comment, "What is this, a chicks' restroom?" if there are more than two dudes waiting to pee; and (3) attempts to shoot his used paper towel into the trash can like a basketball . . . rebounding is optional.

⌒ ARTICLE 34 ⌒

Bros cannot make eye contact during a devil's threeway.

⌒ ARTICLE 35 ⌒

A Bro never rents a chick flick.

⌒ ARTICLE 36 DD ⌒

When questioned in the company of women, a Bro always decries fake breasts.

When in conversation with a woman, fake breasts may arise, but not in the way that you'd like. It's not uncommon for a woman to deftly use trick questions in order to probe a Bro's real thoughts on the subject of breast augmentation.[*] And don't be fooled into thinking your prepared speech on the beauty of the natural human form can get you out of it.

HOW TO HANDLE FAKE BREASTS

> ☒
>
> *Chick:* Ugh, her breasts are so fake.
> *Bro:* Totally. Unnatural is *un*sexy.
> *Chick:* So you've been staring at her breasts, huh?

---

[*] Bigger = better

☒

Chick: Ugh, her breasts are so fake.

Bro: Whose?

Chick: You know who I'm talking about.

Bro: Oh. Yes, those must be fake.

Chick: So you've been staring at her breasts, huh?

☒

Chick: Ugh, her breasts are so fake.

Bro: No?

Chick: *Well, then, why don't you just go marry her, then???*

☑

Chick: Ugh, her breasts are so fake.

Bro: I wouldn't know.

Chick: Oh. Well, they are.

⌒ ARTICLE 37 ⌒

A Bro is under no obligation to open a door for anyone. If women insist on having their own professional basketball league, then they can open their own doors. Honestly, they're not that heavy.

⤚ ARTICLE 38 ⤙

Even in a fight to the death, a Bro never punches another Bro in the groin.

☞ ARTICLE 39 ☜

When a Bro gets a chick's number, he waits at least ninety-six hours before calling her.

SIDE-BRO:
ASK UNCLE BARNEY

Q: *I'm confused—if a woman gives me her phone number, doesn't that mean she wants me to call her? Why do I have to wait so long?*

A: **Broflation**—an unreasonable increase in female expectations about how Bros should act. You call a woman the next day, she tells her friends you called the next day, and soon enough, women everywhere will expect guys to call them the next day. Before you know it, Bros the world over will find themselves trapped in relationships, and all because you couldn't wait ninety-six little hours.

Q: *Okay, I've waited ninety-six hours. When's the best time of day to call?*

A: Call during the middle of the day. You'll have a better chance of catching her voice mail, which ultimately means less conversation. With any luck you'll be able to set something up without ever having to talk to her. Note: Never call after 9 PM—late-night phone calls are the province of the booty call, and only the booty call. See Article 92 for further elaboration.

Q: *I've always heard you wait three days? Why does the Bro Code specify* four?

A: If you've always heard that a Bro should wait three days before calling, you can bet that women have, too. By waiting an extra day, you can make a chick feel special.

⌒ ARTICLE 40 ⌒

Should a Bro become stricken with engagement, his Bros shall stage an intervention and attempt to heal him. This is more commonly known as "a bachelor party."

☞ ARTICLE 41 ☜

A Bro never cries.

EXCEPTIONS: Watching *Field of Dreams*, *E.T.*, or a sports legend retire.*

* Applies only to the first time he retires.

Upon greeting another Bro, a Bro may engage in a high five, fist bump, or Bro hug, but never a full embrace.

EXECUTING A BRO HUG

Step 1:
Interlocking hand clasp

Step 2:
Lean torsos together,
maintaining safe
groin perimeter

Step 3:
One pat on the back

☞ ARTICLE 43 ☜

A Bro loves his country, unless that country isn't America.

≈ ARTICLE 44 ≈

A Bro never applies sunscreen to another Bro.

EXCEPTION: If the Bros are within 7 degrees latitude of the equator.

⤚ ARTICLE 45 ⤙

A Bro never wears jeans to a strip club.

**WHY A BRO NEVER WEARS
JEANS TO A STRIP CLUB**

1. Cloth pockets are roomier and more elastic, allowing for a thicker wad of cash.

2. Denim clashes with a club's leopard, zebra, or other safari animal motif.

3. One word, two syllables, three hours in the ER: zipper.

4. It's a performance, and deserves respect. These erotic dancers have practiced tirelessly on a technically demanding piece of choreographed art. Would you wear dungarees to a ballet?*

5. You don't feel it as much on your kazoo.

---

* Trick question. Bros don't watch ballet.

⮞ ARTICLE 46 ⮜

If a Bro is seated next to some dude who's stuck in the middle seat on an airplane, he shall yield him all of their shared armrest, unless the dude has (a) taken his shoes off, (b) is snoring, (c) makes the Bro get up more than once to use the lavatory, or (d) purchased headphones after they announced the in-flight movie is 27 Dresses. *See Article 35.*

☞ ARTICLE 47 ☜

A Bro never wears pink.
Not even in Europe.

☞ ARTICLE 48 ☜

A Bro never publicly reveals how many chicks he's banged.

COROLLARY: A Bro also never reveals how many chicks *another* Bro has banged.

When a chick meets a Bro, there are three things she wants to know:

1. How much money does he make?
2. Is he shorter than her?
3. How many chicks has he banged?

Eventually, she will figure out the first two, but a Bro never answers the third question. If, however, a Bro feels compelled to answer (i.e., sex is being withheld until he supplies a tally), he can calculate an acceptable number using the following formula:

HOW MANY CHICKS IS IT SAFE FOR A BRO TO SAY HE'S BANGED?

$$n = (a/10 + s)^0 + 5$$

n = number of chicks
a = Bro's age
s = inquiring chick's slut factor (1 = nun, 10 = former nun)

⌒ ARTICLE 49 ⌒

When asked, "Do you need some help?" a Bro shall automatically respond, "I got it," whether or not he's actually got it.

EXCEPTIONS: Carrying an expensive TV, parallel parking an expensive car, loading an expensive TV into an expensive car.

☞ ARTICLE 50 ☜

If a Bro should accidentally strike another Bro's undercarriage with his arm while walking, both Bros silently agree to continue on as if it never happened.

☞ ARTICLE 51 ☜

A Bro checks out another Bro's blind date and reports back with a thumbs-up or thumbs-down.

If you can't get a Bro to scope out your blind date beforehand, there is a way to at least learn how promiscuous she'll be—have her choose the date venue.

BLIND DATE TRANSLATIONS

SHE SUGGESTS ...	PROMISCUITY	SHE'LL BE ...
Dance Club	10	Scantily clad, sweaty, and impossible to hear over the music. A+
Drinks at a Bar	7	A lot of fun, or emotionally unstable . . . promising either way.
Fancy Restaurant	3	Boring. If she expects someone to "pepper her salad" and "refold her napkin," it stands to reason she'll be pretty lifeless in the bedroom.
Meet the Parents	1	Untouchable. But, maybe her mom isn't.
Miniature Golf	5	Way too competitive, or a lesbian . . . and not the hot kind of lesbian.
Church	0 or 10	Looking for marriage, or looking to sin it up before confession. Toss up.

~ ARTICLE 52 ~

A Bro is not required to remember another Bro's birthday, though a phone call every now and again probably wouldn't kill him.

ARTICLE 53

*Even in a drought,
a Bro flushes twice.*

☞ ARTICLE 54 ☜

A Bro is required to go out with his Bros on St. Patty's Day and other official Bro holidays, including Halloween, New Year's Eve, and Desperation Day (February 13).

BROETRY CORNER

There was a young lass from Killarney,
Who promised a gentleman named Arnie,
That she only was his
Though a fat lie this is,
'Cause last night she was screaming "O'Barney."

I was in love with a chick named Pam,
Who showed me pics of her fam,
Pretty cute cat,
But her mom was fat,
So I dumped her that night on the tram.

⁓ ARTICLE 55 ⁓

Even in an emergency that requires a tourniquet, a Bro never borrows from or lends clothes to another Bro.

⌐ ARTICLE 56 ⌐

*A Bro is required to alert another Bro if the **Bro/Chick Ratio** at a party falls below 1:1. However, to avoid **Broflation**, a Bro is only allowed to alert one Bro. Further, a Bro may not speculate on the anticipated Bro/Chick Ratio of a party or venue without first disclosing the present-time observed ratio.*

BRO/CHICK RATIO vs. LIKELIHOOD
OF GETTING ACTION

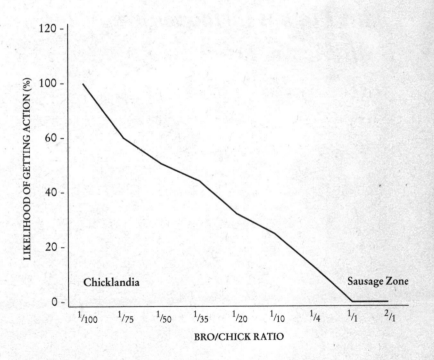

☞ ARTICLE 57 ☜

A Bro never reveals the score of a sporting event to another Bro unless that Bro has thrice confirmed he wants to hear it.

⤳ ARTICLE 58 ⤳

A Bro doesn't grow a mustache.

EXCEPTION: When shaving, it's more than okay for a Bro to keep the whiskers around his mouth until the end so that he might temporarily experiment with different facial hair configurations.

EXCEPTION: Tom Selleck.

☞ ARTICLE 59 ☜

A Bro must always post bail for another Bro, unless it's out of state or, like, crazy expensive.

WHEN IS BAIL CRAZY EXPENSIVE?

Crazy Expensive Bail > (Years You've Been Bros) × $100

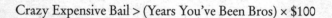

⌒ ARTICLE 60 ⌒

A Bro shall honor thy father and mother, for they were once Bro and chick. However, a Bro never thinks of them in that capacity.

☞ ARTICLE 61 ☜

If a Bro, for whatever reason, becomes aware of another Bro's anniversary with a chick, he shall endeavor to make that information available to his Bro, regardless of whether he thinks his Bro already knows.

Chicks seem to think annual events other than Mardi Gras, the NFL Draft, and the day the swimsuit edition comes out are worthy of celebration. I don't know why, either, but I do know if you become involved with a woman for more than the occasional toss in the hay (which is expressly *not* advised), you'll need to be able to recall certain days of the year with relative accuracy.

DATES THAT CHICKS FIND IMPORTANT

OCCASION	DATE	SHE REMINDS YOU ...
Her birthday	__ / __ / __	Three weeks before, by pointing at jewelry
Anniversary of first date	__ / __ / __	Happily, the day of
Marriage anniversary	__ / __ / __	Angrily, the next day
Children's birthdays	__ / __ / __	At your divorce trial
Grey's Anatomy season premiere	__ / __ / __	In the middle of a playoff game

*In the event that two Bros lock on to the same target, the Bro who calls dibs first has dibs. If both call dibs at the same time, the Bro who counts aloud to ten the fastest has dibs. If both arrive at the number ten at the same time, the Bro who bought the last round of drinks has dibs. If they haven't purchased drinks yet, the taller of the two Bros has dibs. If they're the same height, the Bro with the longer **dry spell** has dibs. Should the dry spells be of equal length, a game of discreet **Broshambo*** shall determine dibs, provided the chick is still there.*

* Rock, paper, scissors for Bros.

← ARTICLE 63 →

A Bro will make any and all efforts to provide his Bro with protection.

Brotection forms a central pillar—or, more accurately, a latex coating for the central pillar—of the Bro way of life. While a Bro is not legally or fiscally responsible for any repercussions of failing to provide protection, it's not uncommon for a Bro to experience pangs of guilt after a fellow Bro becomes infected with a disease, many of which can last an entire lifetime, like when a Bro contracts children.

In the event that one Bro finds himself lacking the prophylactic accoutrements needed to complete the act of coitus in a safe and effective manner, he is in the right to expect another Bro to use all measures within or without his means to provide the aforementioned prophylactic in a timely yet discreet fashion. When a Bro signals his need using previously agreed upon code words and/or body signage, it is understood that his Bro will discontinue all present activity (except the act of coitus itself—whereby the Bro vows to finish as quickly as possible), in order to respond with a panoply of options at the Bro in need's location. A Bro must utilize the most rapid method of transportation available while endeavoring to assist his Bro. In no instance may a bicycle* be used as this is not only humiliating but also potentially harmful to the perineum—a zone of tissue perilously adjacent to the sexual organs. In the event that a state, federal, international, or galactic law is breached due to recklessness, unacceptable levels of speed, and/or the hijacking of airborne vehicle(s), it is understood that the primary Bro will shoulder any associated legal fees or fines. However, any costs or damages incurred from the use of public transportation are the responsibility of the secondary Bro alone as this is an instance of **Quid Pro Bro**. Upon arrival at the primary Bro's location, the secondary Bro must exercise complete discretion so as not to disrupt the primary Bro's "flow," or **Brojo**. Once the primary Bro has been supplied with the necessary prophylactic(s), the **Brocedure** is deemed complete upon exchange of the traditional, though in this case silent, high five. Tacit in this unspoken ritual is the understanding that said episode will never be mentioned again, unless it's part of an awesome story.

* Unless a bicycle is the *only* form of transportation available, like in Southeast Asia or Arkansas or something.

⌒ ARTICLE 64 ⌒

A Bro must provide his Bro with a ticket to an event if said event involves the latter Bro's favorite sports team in a playoff scenario.

☞ ARTICLE 65 ☜

A Bro must always reciprocate a round of drinks among Bros.

EXCEPTION: A Bro is off the hook if his Bro orders a drink that arrives with an umbrella in it.

ARTICLE 66

*If a Bro suffers pain due to the permanent dissolution of a relationship with a lady friend, his Bros shall offer no more than a "that sucks, man" and copious quantities of beer. To eliminate the possibility of any awkward moments in the future, his Bros shall also refrain from any pejorative commentary—deserved or not—regarding said lady friend for a period of three months, when the requisite **backslide window** has fully closed.*

⌒ ARTICLE 67 ⌒

Should a Bro pick up a guitar at a party and commence playing, another Bro shall point out that he is a tool.

⌐ ARTICLE 68 ⌐

If a Bro be on a hot streak, another Bro will do everything possible to ensure its longevity, even if that includes jeopardizing his own personal records, the missing of work, or, if necessary, generating a realistic fear that the end of the world is imminent.

EXCEPTION: Dry spell trumps hot streak.

☙ ARTICLE 69 ☙

Duh.

~ ARTICLE 70 ~

A Bro will drive another Bro to the airport or pick him up, but never both for the same trip. He is not expected to be on time, help with luggage, or inquire about his Bro's trip or general well-being.

⌐ ARTICLE 71 ⌐

As a courtesy to Bros the world over, a Bro never brings more than two other Bros to a party.

**THREE BROS
ARE COOL**

Three Amigos
Three Musketeers

The Police
Apollo 13 Astronauts
Three Stooges
(*Exception*: Hanson)

**FOUR BROS
ARE LAME**

Mount Rushmore
The Fantastic Four
   (feature film version)
The Monkees
Olympic Bobsled Team
Michael Jordan's Teammates
(*Exception*: The Beatles)

BROETRY CORNER

*One Bro makes a solo attack.
A second Bro provides a crutch.
A third Bro rounds out the pack,
But a fourth Bro is one too much.*

~ ARTICLE 72 ~

A Bro never spell-checks.

⌒ ARTICLE 73 ⌒

When a group of Bros are in a restaurant, each shall engage in the time-honored ritual of jockeying to pay the bill, regardless of affordability. When the group ultimately decides to divide the check, each Bro shall act upset rather than enormously relieved.

At a red light, a Bro inches as close as possible to the rear bumper of the car in front of him, and then immediately honks his horn when the light turns green. That way, if another Bro is several cars behind, he'll have a better chance of making it through the intersection before the light turns red again.

⌒ ARTICLE 75 ⌒

A Bro automatically enhances another Bro's job description when introducing him to a chick.

Chicks like to stretch the truth about their age, promiscuity, and sometimes—with the help of extensive makeup and structural lingerie—even their body shape. As such, it's fair game for Bros to exaggerate reality when asked about their **Brofession**. It's also smart: a Bro's career is to a chick what a chick's boobs are to a Bro.

HOW TO INVENT A JOB CHICKS WILL THINK IS HOT

UNIVERSAL CHICK INTERESTS	YOUR JOB
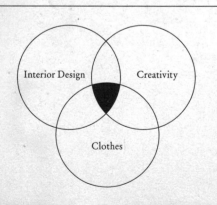	"I invented the walk-in closet."

UNIVERSAL CHICK INTERESTS	YOUR JOB

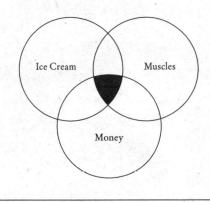

"I'm a muscular ice cream tycoon."

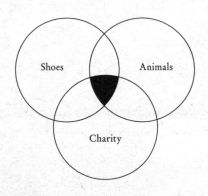

"I design shoes for diabetic cats."

If a Bro is on the phone with a chick while in front of his Bros and, for whatever reason, desires to say "I love you," he shall first excuse himself from the room or employ a subsonic, Barry White–esque tone.

☞ ARTICLE 77 ☜

Bros don't cuddle.

~~EXCEPTION: To conserve body heat in an emergency situation.~~

⌐ ARTICLE 78 ⌐

*A Bro shall never rack jack**
his wingman.

To commemorate and solidify the unbreakable bond between Bro and wingman, it is recommended that before going out, each faces the other, places his left hand on *The Bro Code*, raises his right hand, and recites the Wingman Pledge.

---

* To steal your wingman's chick. Big-time no-no.

THE WINGMAN PLEDGE

I shall uphold the Bro Code to the fullest of my ability.

I will never allow my wingman to go home with less than a six.

I agree to swap rounds of drinks with my wingman,
even if I keep getting stuck paying for shots.

I will never rack jack my wingman, no matter how hot the chick.

I pledge to never leave a wingman behind when invited to a party.

If my wingman meets a hot chick with an ugly
friend, I will **jump on the grenade**.

If my wingman gets rejected by a chick, I shall unequivocally
agree that she sucked anyway, even if I thought she seemed
kind of cool and interesting.

Should my wingman strike up a conversation with a
chick of a questionable legal age, I will endeavor to
ascertain and verify her birth date.

If I discover evidence that my wingman's chick is in a
relationship, I shall make that information available to him,
unless it's pretty clear the boyfriend/husband isn't there.

I shall honor and respect the dibs system.

⌒ ARTICLE 79 ⌒

*At a wedding, Bros shall reluctantly trudge out for the garter toss and feign interest for the benefit of the chicks present. Whichever Bro gets stuck with the garter shall lightheartedly pretend he's not horrified at the thought of being the next one to drop before scurrying to the bar for a very stiff drink and/or shots.**

COROLLARY: If a Bro's date should catch the bouquet, he shall act excited (if he wishes to sleep with her ever again) before scurrying to the bar to join the garter Bro for a very stiff drink and/or shots.

* Open bar only.

⁀ ARTICLE 80 ⁀

A Bro shall make every effort to aid another Bro in riding the tricycle, short of completing the tricycle himself.*

RULES FOR RIDING THE TRICYCLE

1. The aggregate age of all three participants shall not exceed eighty-three years.

2. The aggregate weight of all three participants shall be less than 400 pounds/181.44 kg.

3. No money or other considerations may be exchanged for services rendered.

4. Pregnant women shall consult with their physician before riding the tricycle.

5. No wheel of the tricycle shall be within three branches of another's family tree.

6. No black-soled sneakers.

7. Female participants shall refrain from destroying the illusion that this is new to them.

8. Kitchen appliances and other electrical devices are strictly forbidden.

9. Participants must shower before riding the tricycle, and definitely after.

---

* Engaging in a threesome.

~ ARTICLE 81 ~

A Bro leaves the toilet seat up
for his Bros.

~ ARTICLE 82 ~

If two Bros get into a heated argument over something and one says something out of line, the other shall not expect him to "take it back" or "apologize" to make amends. That's inhuman.

☞ ARTICLE 83 ☜

A Bro shall, at all costs, honor the Platinum Rule: Never, ever, ever, ever "love" thy neighbor. In particular, a Bro shall never mix it up romantically with a co-worker.

EXCEPTIONS

- Co-worker is an eight or better

- You are co-worker's superior

- Co-worker dresses a little slutty

- Getting fired from job not such a bad thing

- Company recently sued for sexual harassment— unlikely to happen again

- Someone makes a bet that you can't

- You are switching floors soon

- You and co-worker get stuck in elevator

- You hit the emergency button and get "stuck" in the elevator with co-worker

- Co-worker going to be fired, or soon will be, after you sabotage co-worker's files

- You mixed it up with co-worker before becoming co-workers

- Co-worker hits on you

- You are in a little bit of a rut, romantically speaking

- Co-worker going through divorce

- Co-worker looking pretty good lately

- Co-worker not offended when you "accidentally" email provocative pictures of self to office

☞ ARTICLE 84 ☜

A Bro shall stop whatever he's doing and watch Die Hard *if it's on TV.*

COROLLARY: Ditto *The Shawshank Redemption.*

COROLLARY: Also *Top Gun*, *The Big Lebowski*, and the first half of *Full Metal Jacket.*

COROLLARY: And porn. Duh.

⌐ ARTICLE 85 ⌐

If a Bro buys a new car, he is required to pop the hood when showing it off to his Bros.

COROLLARY: His Bros are required to whistle, even if they have no idea what they're whistling at.

⌐ ARTICLE 86 ⌐

When a Bro meets a chick, he shall endeavor to find out where she fits on the Hot/Crazy Scale before pursuing her.

The theory of evolution alleges that men evolved from monkeys . . . but what about women? It seems that as men became less hairy, more upright, and less interested in throwing their own poo, women became more attractive but somehow *more* crazy.

Today's chicks like to straddle the line between hot and crazy: the hotter they are, the crazier they are; the crazier they are, the hotter they seem. All of this is confusing to a Bro and, very often, dangerous. How is a Bro to know whether a chick is hot and crazy in a "let's duck into the bathroom" kind of way, or hot and crazy in a "let's huff paint and stalk your ex-girlfriends" kind of way?

Fortunately, I've devised a test that allows Bros to quickly determine where a chick fits on the Hot/Crazy Scale. Answer yes or no to each question in the columns, add up your "yes" answers, and then plot the coordinates on the Hot/Crazy Scale. Ideally, your chick is right on the line, but if she's anywhere above it, run away.

HOT vs. CRAZY

HOT	YES	NO
Likes to sing aloud to Poison songs		
Can name a player from every NFL team		
Exhibits some daddy issues		
Plays with the hair on her head		
Full of wild animal magnetism		
Squeezes your leg while talking		
Wears a slinky dress		
Softly kisses you good night		
Blinks her eyes at you seductively		
HOT Coordinate		

CRAZY	YES	NO
Likes to sing aloud about poison		
Has served time with a player from every NFL team		
Exhibits some daddy issues		
Shaves the hair on her head		
Apartment full of wild animals		
Squeezes your face while talking		
Wears a Slinky		
Softly stabs you in the neck		
Has never once blinked at you		
CRAZY Coordinate		

THE HOT/CRAZY SCALE

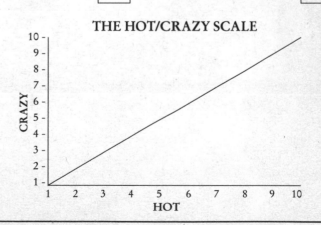

113

⌒ ARTICLE 87 ⌒

*A Bro never questions another
Bro's stated golf score, maximum
bench press, or height. He can,
however, ask the Bro to prove it,
traditionally in the form of a wager.*

⌒ ARTICLE 88 ⌒

*If a Bro, for whatever reason,
must drive another Bro's car, he
shall not adjust the preprogrammed
radio stations, the mirrors, or the seat
position, even if this last requirement
results in the Bro trying to drive
the vehicle as a giant praying
mantis would.*

☞ ARTICLE 89 ☜

A Bro shall always say yes in support of a Bro.

When out and about, you must be prepared to affirm anything a Bro tells a chick. "Yes, he's single." "Yes, we're Navy SEALs." "Yes, he invented Facebook." While this usually entails stretching the truth about personal wealth, athletic prowess, or the ability to operate various aircraft, on occasion you'll be required to pretend you're from out of town. If you can stomach dressing up like someone's dad, pretending to be a tourist in your own hometown is a great way to score chicks . . . if you're ready with a believable backstory.

HOW TO SOUND LIKE A TOURIST

Hi, I'm _____ _____ . I'm from _____ _____ ,
      (real first name) (bird of prey)   (compass direction) (biblical locale)

_____ . Go, Fightin' _____! Yep, it was a great
(Midwestern or rectangular state)   (woodland creatures)

place to grow up. Walking down Main Street at _____ , and dropping
                                     (time of day)

in at _____ 's for some homemade _____ , well, it
   (three-letter male name)   (diabetic dessert)

makes my eyes water and my tummy grumble just thinking about it,

yessiree. From time to time I like to check in on ol' Mrs. _____ ,
                                       (tree species)

bless her heart, and her prize-winning _____ _____ .
                       (color)   (plural vegetable)

My high school sweetheart _____ and I used to neck up on
                   (flower type)

_____ _____ Point. Thought we'd get married but
(dangerous animal) (body of water)

the good Lord had other plans for her in the form of a _____
                                     (American sedan)

losing control round _____ 's Curve. After she passed, I took
              (American president)

up _____ whittling to ease the pain, but, golly, I sure don't
 (piece of furniture)

meet many ladies in that line of work, specially not ones as pretty as

you. Gosh, you're prettier than a _____ on a(n) _____ day,
                         (barnyard animal)   (season)

glistening in the _____ shine.
          (celestial body)

ARTICLE 90

A Bro shows up at another Bro's party with at least one more unit of alcohol than he plans to drink. So if a Bro plans on chugging a six-pack, he shall bring a six-pack plus at least one can of beer. If the party sucks and/or there are too many dudes, the Bro is entitled to leave with his alcohol, though etiquette dictates he should wait until nobody is looking.

ARTICLE 91

If a group of Bros suspect that their Bro is trying to give himself a nickname, they shall rally to call him by an adjacent yet more demeaning nickname.

A Bro keeps his booty calls at a safe distance.

To maintain the purity of such a beautiful, impersonal, and vapid relationship, a Bro never becomes emotionally attached to his booty call.

HOW TO KEEP A BOOTY CALL A BOOTY CALL

DON'T	WHY?
Buy her anything . . . not even a drink.	Gifts imply consideration and forethought—a booty call should never feel like more than a reflexive impulse, like a sneeze or a gag.
Refer to your booty call as your "booty call."	Some human beings—particularly women—like to think there's more to sex than sex.
Stick around after sex.	A booty call is strictly business. Once the transaction has taken place, anything else is superfluous, inefficient, and awkward.
Call again if your booty call doesn't respond that night.	Two calls imply something bad has happened: like you've been diagnosed with an STD or want to take her out on a date.
Call more than twice a month.	In some countries, this is considered marriage.
Think about her before midnight.	Idle thoughts can lead to a relationship.
Agree to meet on any other night than when you call.	That is called a date.

⁓ ARTICLE 93 ⁔

Bros don't speak French to one another.

ARTICLE 94

If a Bro is in the bathroom and runs out of toilet paper, another Bro may toss him a new roll, but at no point may their hands touch or the door open more than 30 degrees.

~ ARTICLE 95 ~

A Bro shall alert another Bro to the presence of a chesty woman, regardless of whether or not he knows the Bro. Such alerts may not be administered verbally.

HOW TO SIGNAL WHEN BOOBS ARE PRESENT

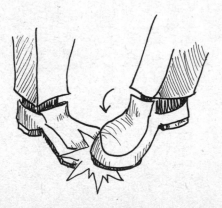

THE SHOE TAP—To be avoided in public restrooms

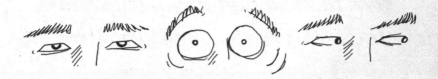

THE EYE REDIRECT

THE SWIFT SHIN KICK—D cups and up only, please

ARTICLE 96

Bros shall go camping once a year, or at least attempt to start a fire.

NOTE: Attempt to start a fire *out*side.

☞ ARTICLE 97 ☜

Where a Bro went to college is going to kick his Bro's college's ass all over the field this weekend.

⌐ ARTICLE 98 ⌐

A Bro never lies to his Bros about the hotness of chicks at a given social venue or event.

SIDE-BRO: THE BRO WHO CRIED "HOT CHICKS"

There once lived a Bro who would text his Bros: "Hot chicks in the bar tonight!" When his Bros would arrive to wingman him, he would laugh at them for there were no hot chicks, just, like, a lot of dudes or something. The Bro did this a couple of times because he thought it was hysterical—and it kind of is—until one night he walked into the bar to discover a Hawaiian Tropic calendar shoot taking place. The Bro texted his Bros in terror: "Dudes, seriously need a wingman right now . . . hot-chick calendar shoot!" But this time his Bros paid no heed to his cry, nor did they leave their video game marathon to assist him. The Bro tried to score a bikini babe on his own, but with no wingman, he was torn to pieces by the entire flock.

There is no believing a Bro who lies about hot chicks, even when he speaks the truth.

~ ARTICLE 99 ~

A Bro never asks for directions when lost.

EXCEPTION: A Bro may ask for directions from a hot chick who seems to know the area.

EXCEPTION: A Bro may ask for directions from a hot chick even if she also appears lost.

EXCEPTION: A Bro may ask for directions from a hot chick even if he is not lost at all.

⌐ ARTICLE 100 ⌐

When pulling up to a stoplight, a Bro lowers his window so that all might enjoy his music selection.

COROLLARY: If there happens to be a hot chick driving the car next to the Bro, the Bro shall pull his sunglasses down to get a better look. If he's not wearing his sunglasses, he will first put them on, then pull them down to get a better look.

⌐ ARTICLE 101 ⌐

If a Bro asks another Bro to keep a secret, he shall take that secret to his grave. This is what makes them Bros, not chicks.*

NOTE: A woman's lust for gossip is matched only by her passion to have babies and accessorize. As such, a Bro should take heed when divulging a secret to a married Bro.

* And beyond, if the Bro discovers there is indeed life after death.

☞ ARTICLE 102 ☜

A Bro shall take great care in selecting and training his wingman.

WINGMAN APPLICATION

Name: _____

Alias: _____
     (e.g., Jack Package, the Barnacle)

Special Skills:
     (e.g., PowerPoint, speak German, masseur)

On the scale below, please rate your attractiveness.

1——2——3——4——5——6——7——8——9——Barney Stinson

Multiple Choice

1. You are the sessions drummer for Van Halen. Who is not your lead singer?

   a. David Lee Roth
   b. Gary Cherone
   c. Sammy Hagar
   d. Barney Stinson

2. Historically, a chick does not enjoy jokes about her:

   a. face
   b. shoes
   c. intelligence
   d. none of the above

Short Answer

You are character A. Character B is your wingman. Explain what game you would run and why.

_____

_____

_____

Essay Question

On the back of this application, write about a person who has made a significant impact on your life.

_____

＾ ARTICLE 103 ＾

A Bro never wears socks with sandals. He commits to one cohesive footgear plan and sticks with it.

ARTICLE 104

The mom of a Bro is always off-limits. But the stepmom of a Bro is fair game if she initiates and/or is wearing at least one article of leopard print clothing . . . provided she looks good in it . . . but not if she smokes menthol cigarettes.

Be it here resolved that at no point is it permissible for one Bro to engage in carnal delicacies with another Bro's mother. It is, however, allowed and encouraged for one Bro to graphically suggest to a Bro the athletic feats, animalia, and/or machinery utilized during a fictional encounter with his mom. (Nota bene: It is customary for a Bro to avoid such **Brocularity** if his Bro's mom is a nine or better, for fear of Oedipal inducement.) Should a Bro discover his Bro is adopted, he is free to pursue his Bro's adoptive mother, but only after first corroborating nonbiological parentage through notarized birth certificates, hospital records, or comparative deoxyribonucleic acid gel electrophoresis, whichever is most convenient.

If a Bro is not invited to another Bro's wedding, he doesn't make a big deal out of it, even if, let's face it, he was kind of responsible for setting up the couple and had already picked out the perfect wedding gift and everything. It's cool. No big whoop.

ARTICLE 106

*Given an option on quantity when
ordering a beer with his Bros,
a Bro always selects the largest
size available or shall never hear
the end of it that night.*

⌐ ARTICLE 107 ⌐

A Bro never leaves another Bro hanging.

Besides the obvious health hazards inherent in keeping an arm aloft for an extended period of time, the emotional effects of leaving a Bro out to dry in public can be devastating. If you ever see a Bro, even one you don't know, looking around frantically with a paw held high in the air, throw him a **Brone** and hit him up top.

COMMON BRO FIVES

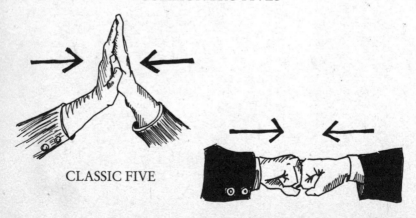

CLASSIC FIVE

THE FIST BUMP

THE EXPLODING FIST BUMP

AROUND THE WORLD

THE SELF FIVE

THE RELAPSE FIVE

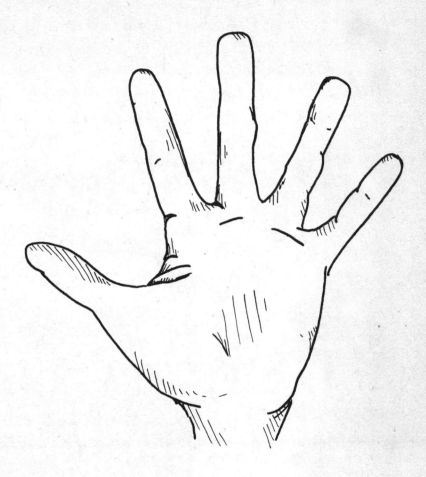

BRO CODE FIVE!
(tear this one out and carry it with you
so you'll never be left hanging . . .)

⌁ ARTICLE 108 ⌁

*If a Bro forgets a guy's name,
he may call him "brah," "dude,"
or "man," but never "Bro."*

⌒ ARTICLE 109 ⌒

When Bros attend a sporting event and see themselves on the JumboTron, they shall purse their lips and flex their biceps while informing the crowd that their team is number one, despite any objective rankings to the contrary.

☞ ARTICLE 110 ☜

If a Bro is hitting it off with a chick, his Bro shall do anything within his means to ensure the desired outcome.

You and your Bros will undoubtedly face many seemingly insurmountable challenges on your quest to score a one-night stand. Here are some techniques to make them mountable.

TROUBLESHOOTING THE ONE-NIGHT STAND

PROBLEM	FIX
I forgot her name	Have a Bro introduce himself and listen closely. Note: Choose your ugliest Bro.
She rejected my drink offer	Offer her breakfast in bed as an alternative. If she doesn't acquiesce, say you were kidding.
She's having a girls' night out	Identify and target the reason for the girls' night out—the recently dumped chick
The lights came on— she's ugly	Squint hard. If she asks what you're doing, say you forgot your glasses or you're just deeply concerned about the environment or something

If a Bro discovers another Bro has forgotten to sign out of his email, the Bro will sign out for him, but only after first sending a few angry emails to random contacts and then deleting all sent messages.

⌒ ARTICLE 112 ⌒

A Bro doesn't sing along to music in a bar.

EXCEPTION: A Bro may participate in karaoke.

EXCEPTION TO EXCEPTION: No chick songs.

☞ ARTICLE 113 ☜

A Bro abides by the accepted age-difference formula when pursuing a younger chick.

ACCEPTABLE AGE-DIFFERENCE FORMULA

$$x \leq y/2 + 7$$

x = chick's age; y = Bro's age

This formula limits crafty old-timers from scooping up all the younger hotties, while also preventing Bros from seeing a crusty old man with a hot chick and being forced to imagine them getting it on in his adjustable bed.

AGE-DIFFERENCE REFERENCE CHART (for your wallet)

Bro	Chick	Bro	Chick	Bro	Chick	Bro	Chick	Bro	Chick	Bro	Chick
22	18	36	25	50	32	64	39	78	46	92	53
23	18.5	37	25.5	51	32.5	65	39.5	79	46.5	93	53.5
24	19	38	26	52	33	66	40	80	47	94	54
25	19.5	39	26.5	53	33.5	67	40.5	81	47.5	95	54.5
26	20	40	27	54	34	68	41	82	48	96	55
27	20.5	41	27.5	55	34.5	69	heh	83	48.5	97	55.5
28	21	42	28	56	35	70	42	84	49	98	56
29	21.5	43	28.5	57	35.5	71	42.5	85	49.5	99	56.5
30	22	44	29	58	36	72	43	86	50	100	57
31	22.5	45	29.5	59	36.5	73	43.5	87	50.5		
32	23	46	30	60	37	74	44	88	51		
33	23.5	47	30.5	61	37.5	75	44.5	89	51.5		
34	24	48	31	62	38	76	45	90	52		
35	24.5	49	31.5	63	38.5	77	45.5	91	52.5		

⌐ ARTICLE 114 ⌐

If a Bro must crash on his Bro's couch for an extended period of time, he shall offer to split the cost of toilet paper and the cable bill if said period exceeds two weeks. If he stays longer than a month, he shall offer to contribute some rent. If he stays longer than two months, he shall steam clean the couch or have it incinerated, whichever is more applicable.

*A "clothing optional" beach
doesn't really mean "clothing
optional" for Bros.*

❧ ARTICLE 116 ❧

A Bro shall not kill another Bro or a Bro's chances to score with a chick.

Every Bro is endowed with a right to life and a right to pursue hot chicks. Violating either of these God-given rights is a heinous offense that could result in the strictest penalty recognized in the Bro Code: loss of permanent shotgun status.

ARTICLE 117

A Bro never willingly relinquishes possession of a remote control. If another Bro desires a channel change, he may verbally request one or engage in the fool's errand of getting up to manually change the channel.

COROLLARY: It is fully expected a Bro will try anything to gain possession of the remote, up to and including an attempt to flatulently smoke his Bro(s) out of the room.

⌒ ARTICLE 118 ⌒

When a Bro is with his Bros,
he is not a vegetarian.

ARTICLE 119

*When three Bros must share the backseat of a car, it is unacceptable for any Bro to put his arm around another Bro to increase space. Likewise, it is unacceptable for two Bros to share a motorcycle, unless said motorcycle is equipped with a sidecar . . . a **Brotorcycle**.*

~ ARTICLE 120 ~

A Bro always calls another Bro by his last name.

EXCEPTION: If a Bro's last name is also a racial epithet.

◞ ARTICLE 121 ◟

Even if he's never skied before, a Bro doesn't trifle with the bunny slope.

COROLLARY: If a Bro experiences a catastrophic wipeout, he can always blame his bindings or the "conditions."

☞ ARTICLE 122 ☜

A Bro is always psyched. Always.

If you're having trouble getting psyched, or you need to get a Bro psyched, you can always make yourself a "Get Psyched" mix.

CLASSIC "GET PSYCHED SONGS"

"You Give Love a Bad Name"
—Bon Jovi

"I Wanna Rock" —Twisted Sister

"The Humpty Dance"
—Digital Underground

"Don't Stop Believin'" —Journey

"You're the Best Around"
—Joe Esposito

"Lick It Up" —KISS

"Paradise City" —Guns N' Roses

"Tom Sawyer" —Rush

"The Transformers Theme"
—Vince DiCola with
    Optimus Prime

"Dancing with Myself"
—Billy Idol

"Rock You Like a Hurricane"
—Scorpions

"Come Sail Away"—Styx

"Free Bird" (second half only)
—Lynyrd Skynyrd

"Panama" —Van Halen

"Jessie's Girl" —Rick Springfield

"Talk Dirty to Me" —Poison

"Thunderstruck" —AC/DC

"High Enough"
—Damn Yankees

"Hip Hop Hooray"
—Naughty By Nature

"Dr. Feelgood" —Mötley Crüe

"Round and Round" —Ratt

⌇ ARTICLE 123 ⌇

Two Bros shall maintain at least a three-foot radius between them while dancing on the same floor, even when reenacting the knife fight from "Beat It," which, I guess, two Bros shouldn't do anyway, or at least not very often.

⌐ ARTICLE 124 ⌐

*If a Bro should shoot an air ball,
strike out while playing softball, or
throw a gutter ball while **Browling**,
he is required to make some sort
of excuse for himself.*

If a Bro is driving ahead of another Bro in a Bro Train, he is required to attempt to lose him in traffic as a funny joke.

ARTICLE 126

In a scenario where two or more Bros are watching entertainment of the adult variety, one Bro is forbidden from intentionally or unintentionally touching another Bro in ANY capacity. This may include but is not limited to: the high five, the fist bump, or the congratulatory gluteal pat. Winking is also kind of a no-no.

PRE–STRIP CLUB CHECKLIST

❏ Converted sufficient funds to singles in the local currency.

❏ Hid ATM and credit cards deep in wallet yet still accessible in case of rare "twins" scenario.

❏ Got drunk.

❏ Planted fake "movie producer" business cards on person where they might "accidentally" fall out into cleavage of dancer(s).

❏ Pledged to avoid dancers with names like Smokey, Hepatitia, and Thunder.

❏ Turned off heat/AC in apartment, saving both utility costs *and* the environment.

❏ Not wearing jeans.

❏ Read in-depth synopsis of movie girlfriend thinks you're going to see.

ARTICLE 127

*A Bro will always help another
Bro reconstruct the events from the
previous night, unless those events
entail hooking up with an ugly
chick or the Bro repeatedly saying
"I love you, man" to all his Bros.*

MAC—Memory Assistance and/or Correction—often comes into
play around the holidays because when people gather together
with loved ones, the need to drink alcohol increases exponentially.

Halloween is a time when Bros are especially susceptible to
memory loss due to the lethal combination of abundant sweet things,
liquor, and of course, candy. In fact, one year I awoke with four new
phone numbers but no idea who gave them to me. Fortunately, based
on the times I saved the numbers into my phone and a few hazy
memories of the four different costumes I wore at the party the night
before, I was able to create a logic matrix.

I dressed up as a Viking, a ninja, Teddy Roosevelt, and of course
my old standby, Gandhi, and in each costume I picked up a different
chick: a slutty nun, a slutty Cinderella, a slutty slut, and a slutty some-
kind-of-creature with ears and a tail.

To work the puzzle, put an "X" in the box when you've ruled it out based on the clues. For example, Clue 1 says I didn't wake up in my ninja costume, so the Ninja/2:21 AM box is already crossed out. *Hint*: Some clues will allow you to put an "X" in more than one box.

WHAT I REMEMBERED

1. I didn't wake up in my ninja costume, but I know I ended the night with some tail.
2. The slutty slut was gone by November 1, so she missed my scrumptious Gandhi . . . she too would go hungry.
3. Both Cinderella and the nun were intrigued by my sword. I was still seeing throwing stars as I changed into my Viking costume.
4. When I first entered the party, I spoke softly to hotties and showed them my "big stick." Politically speaking of course—I was dressed as Teddy Roosevelt.
5. I got Cinderella's number early. I was afraid her melons would turn into pumpkins at midnight.

	Slutty Cinderella	Slutty Slut	Slutty Ears/Tail	Slutty Nun	9:42 PM	10:56 PM	12:03 AM	2:21 AM	
Viking									9:42 PM
Roosevelt									10:56 PM
Ninja								X	12:03 AM
Gandhi									2:21 AM
9:42 PM									
10:56 PM									
12:03 AM									
2:21 AM									

See answers on page 195.

⌒ ARTICLE 128 ⌒

A Bro never wears two articles of clothing at the same time that bear the same school name, vacation destination, or sports team. Even in a laundry emergency, it's preferred that a Bro go out half naked rather than violate this code ... half naked from the waist up, naturally.

If a Bro lends another Bro a DVD, video game, or piece of lawn machinery, he shall not expect to ever get it back, unless his Bro happens to die and bequeath it back to him.

⌐ ARTICLE 130 ⌐

*If a Bro learns another Bro has
been in a traffic accident, he
must first ask what type of car he
collided with and whether
it got totaled before asking
if his Bro is okay.*

⤝ ARTICLE 131 ⤞

While a Bro is not expected to know exactly how to change a tire, he is required to at least drag out the jack and stare at the flat for a while. If he needs to consult the car's ownership manual to locate the jack, he shall do so from inside the car, where he is not visible to passersby and where he can discreetly call a tow truck, after which it is recommended that he hide the jack by the side of the road so he'll have a legitimate excuse when the tow truck arrives.

⌐ ARTICLE 132 ⌐

If a Bro decides to let all of his Bros down and get married, he is required to invite them to the wedding, even if this directly violates the wishes of his fiancée and results in a "no sex" penalty or whatever lame domestic punishment couples might employ.

A bride thinks of her wedding day as the happiest day of her life. A groom thinks of his wedding day as the saddest: his marriage signifies the death of Broing out with his Bros. But there's a simple way for the groom to send his Bros out with a bang . . . bridesmaids.

Squeezed into ugly identical dresses, bridesmaids have one goal: to get out of them. Studies have shown that a cocktail of jealousy, Bros in formal wear, and well, cocktails make a bridesmaid one of the most accessible chicks on the planet.

ARTICLE 133

A Bro only claims a fart after first accusing at least one other Bro.

EXCEPTION: "Pull my finger."

ARTICLE 134

A Bro is entitled to use a woman as his wingman.

Since the dawn of man, Bros have spoken in hushed tones about a wingman with powers so awesome, one wink could summon a dozen hotties to your side. I'm speaking, of course, about the **wingwoman**. Think of it—if your wingman already knows what women want to hear, isn't that an advantage far greater than having a lot of money, a full head of hair, or even a speedboat? Yes, and the best part is that wingwomen do exist. To acquire one, though, you'll need to overcome the sexist misconceptions that so often scare chicks away from helping Bros bang other chicks.

THE WINGWOMAN: TRUE OR FALSE?

A wingwoman has to pee too much.	**False** A chick's bladder is smaller but easier to control. How else can a theaterful of chicks sit through *The Lake House*?
A wingwoman never buys drinks.	**True** But your expenses are offset by other dudes buying her drinks.
A wingwoman is distracted by gossip.	**False** What Bros see as just high-pitched prattle, women read as a complex discussion held secretly in body language.
A wingwoman will seem like my girlfriend.	**True** But *nothing* attracts women more than a dude *with* a girlfriend.

ARTICLE 135

If a scenario arises in which a Bro has promised two of his Bros permanent shotgun, one of the following shall determine the copilot: (1) foot race to the car, (2) silent auction, or in the case of a road trip exceeding 450 miles, (3) a no-holds-barred cage match to the death.

☞ ARTICLE 136 ☜

When interrogated by a girlfriend about a bachelor party, a Bro shall offer nothing more than an uninterested "It was okay."

COROLLARY: A Bro never brings a camera to a bachelor party. The only memento a Bro is allowed to bring home from a bachelor party is one that can only be destroyed by penicillin.

☞ ARTICLE 137 ☜

When hosting, a Bro orders enough pizza for all his Bros.

THE PIZZA EQUATION

$$p = \frac{3b}{8}$$

p = number of pizzas (rounded up to nearest integer)
b = number of Bros (including yourself)

Equation assumes Bro hunger coefficient (h):

$$h(b) = \frac{m}{\Delta t}$$

m = gravitational mass of the Bro
Δt = time elapsed since Bro last ate

Equation assumes no hunger rate of change, which is fully expressed in Stinson's Pizza Integral:

$$p\,(b) = \int_{b}^{\infty} \frac{\{1 + [b\,/(b+1)]\} \times 3.4}{8}$$

ARTICLE 138

A real Bro doesn't laugh when a guy gets hit in the groin.

EXCEPTION: Unless he doesn't know the guy.

ARTICLE 139

Regardless of veracity, a Bro never admits familiarity with a Broadway show or musical, despite the fact that, yes, "Broadway" begins with "Bro."

⌒ ARTICLE 140 ⌒

A Bro reserves the right to simply walk away during the first five minutes of a date.

THE LEMON LAW

The Lemon Law is a little-known dating loophole that allows a Bro to bail on any date in the first five minutes, no questions asked. How many times has a Bro set you up with a blind date who winds up looking like the unmasked Predator? Now, with the Lemon Law, you no longer need to sit through that kind of torture or waste any of the Predator's time. Simply present your date with a Lemon Law card, and you're out the door.

I'M SORRY, BUT THIS DATE IS OVER

IN ACCORDANCE WITH
THE LEMON LAW
www.barneysblog.com

The *Lemon Law* may be invoked if, at any point during the initial five minutes (300 seconds) of a first date, either party deems the union hopeless and elects to abort said date in the interest of time and/or self-respect. Receipt of this card hereby absolves the **giver** from any "hard feelings" or "questions" from the **lemon lawyee** relevant to the discontinuance of the date, which may be terminated for any reason including, but not limited to: tawdry attire, breath, homeliness, misplaced/excessive body hair, Long Island accent, public school education, bad credit, no credit, suspicious odor(s).

ADDENDA
(I) **giver** may waive the *Lemon Law* should **lemon lawyee** immediately consent to a no-strings attached "stand," duration of which shall be no longer than one (1) night. (II) the terms of this agreement are non-exclusively transferable, in deference to the emergence of the Lemon Law as a "thing." (III) in the unlikely event of a simultaneous invocation, parties shall enact one (1) "high five," with neither party officially assuming credit for the Lemon Law issuance.

I'M SORRY, BUT THIS DATE IS OVER

IN ACCORDANCE WITH
THE LEMON LAW
www.barneysblog.com

The *Lemon Law* may be invoked if, at any point during the initial five minutes (300 seconds) of a first date, either party deems the union hopeless and elects to abort said date in the interest of time and/or self-respect. Receipt of this card hereby absolves the **giver** from any "hard feelings" or "questions" from the **lemon lawyee** relevant to the discontinuance of the date, which may be terminated for any reason including, but not limited to: tawdry attire, breath, homeliness, misplaced/excessive body hair, Long Island accent, public school education, bad credit, no credit, suspicious odor(s).

ADDENDA
(I) **giver** may waive the *Lemon Law* should **lemon lawyee** immediately consent to a no-strings attached "stand," duration of which shall be no longer than one (1) night. (II) the terms of this agreement are non-exclusively transferable, in deference to the emergence of the Lemon Law as a "thing." (III) in the unlikely event of a simultaneous invocation, parties shall enact one (1) "high five," with neither party officially assuming credit for the Lemon Law issuance.

I'M SORRY, BUT THIS DATE IS OVER

IN ACCORDANCE WITH
THE LEMON LAW
www.barneysblog.com

The *Lemon Law* may be invoked if, at any point during the initial five minutes (300 seconds) of a first date, either party deems the union hopeless and elects to abort said date in the interest of time and/or self-respect. Receipt of this card hereby absolves the **giver** from any "hard feelings" or "questions" from the **lemon lawyee** relevant to the discontinuance of the date, which may be terminated for any reason including, but not limited to: tawdry attire, breath, homeliness, misplaced/excessive body hair, Long Island accent, public school education, bad credit, no credit, suspicious odor(s).

ADDENDA
(I) **giver** may waive the *Lemon Law* should **lemon lawyee** immediately consent to a no-strings attached "stand," duration of which shall be no longer than one (1) night. (II) the terms of this agreement are non-exclusively transferable, in deference to the emergence of the Lemon Law as a "thing." (III) in the unlikely event of a simultaneous invocation, parties shall enact one (1) "high five," with neither party officially assuming credit for the Lemon Law issuance.

ARTICLE 141

A Bro can only get a manicure if (a) he's trying to sleep with the hot Asian woman performing the manicure, or (b) it's been longer than a month since his last manicure. It's called the Bro Code, not the Slob Code.

∽ ARTICLE 142 ∼

A Bro shall seek no revenge if he passes out around his Bros and wakes up to find marker all over his face.

When executing a high five, a Bro is forbidden from intertwining fingers or grasping his Bro's hand.

BROETRY CORNER

"Hai-Five-Ku"

One two three four five
Raise each one high in the air
Smack and release, Bro

❦ ARTICLE 144 ❧

It is unacceptable for two Bros to share a hotel bed without first exhausting all couch, cot, and pillows-on-floor combinations. If it's still unavoidable, they shall prevent any incidental spoonage by arm wrestling* to determine who sleeps under the covers. Once decided, each Bro shall don as many lower layers as possible before silently fist bumping the other good night.

* Not on the bed.

⇜ ARTICLE 145 ⇝

A Bro is never offended if another Bro fails to return a phone call, text, or email in a timely fashion.

⮀ ARTICLE 146 ⮀

A Bro refrains from using too much detail when relating sexual exploits to his Bros.

Providing graphic detail when describing a sexual feat unconsciously forces your Bros to picture you naked . . . and there's no coming back from that.

HOW DETAILED CAN YOU GET?

LEVEL	SAMPLE DIALOGUE	ACCEPTABLE?
Vague	"Got laid last night."	👍
Moderate	"Totally got laid last night."	👍
Specific	"She put her [censored] on my [censored], which made my [censored] [censored] [censored]ly."	👎 👎

☞ ARTICLE 147 ☜

If a Bro sees another Bro get into a fight, he immediately has his Bro's back.

EXCEPTION: If his Bro has picked a fight with a scary-looking guy.

EXCEPTION: If this is the third fight (or more) his Bro has gotten into that week.

EXCEPTION: If the Bro has a note from a physician excusing him from having anybody's back.

A Bro doesn't listen to chick music . . . in front of other Bros. When alone, a Bro may listen to, say, a Sarah McLachlan album or two, but only to gain valuable insights into the female psyche, not because he finds her melodies tragically haunting yet curiously uplifting at the same time.

ARTICLE 149

A Bro pretends to understand and enjoy cigars.

CIGAR WORD SEARCH

```
A  C  H  U  R  C  H  I  L  L  B  O
F  F  G  E  T  O  B  A  C  C  O  L
I  E  W  P  S  C  J  G  O  R  U  X
C  Z  T  R  C  T  T  L  T  W  Q  Y
I  R  L  E  W  I  N  S  K  Y  U  R
O  M  H  S  B  R  A  F  T  U  E  R
N  T  U  I  B  C  B  R  O  Q  T  I
A  E  M  D  L  G  U  S  V  T  E  L
D  R  I  E  E  Y  C  U  T  T  E  R
O  U  D  N  M  A  T  R  K  V  H  N
P  I  O  T  L  J  W  K  O  Z  R  Y
F  R  R  E  N  H  Y  E  Y  L  R  Z
```

- ❏ Tobacco
- ❏ Churchill
- ❏ Bouquet
- ❏ Lewinsky
- ❏ Humidor
- ❏ Fidel Castro
- ❏ Cuban
- ❏ Cutter
- ❏ Presidente
- ❏ Aficionado

ARTICLE 150

No sex with your Bro's ex.

I t is never, ever permissible for a Bro to sleep with his Bro's ex. Violating this code is worse than killing a Bro.

AMENDMENTS

AMENDMENT I

A Bro is entitled to have sex with his Bro's ex if she initiates it, she is really hot, or his Bro is out of town or in a different room.

AMENDMENT II

If a Bro writes and directs a trilogy of awesome space-themed sagas that define a generation's childhood, he is forbidden from later tarnishing that legacy by crapping out a prequel trilogy that forces Bros to specify "Episodes 4 to 6" or "the *real* trilogy" when referencing what was once a perfect series of movies, regardless of how anyone feels about Ewoks.

AMENDMENT III

Should a Bro become aware that his Bro has a *really* hot sister (a nine or higher), she is no longer protected under Article 19: A Bro shall not sleep with another Bro's sister. That said, a Bro should reevaluate if the sister kind of resembles his Bro in a wig.

AMENDMENT IV

A Bro shall never turn away a Bro who shows up uninvited at his door with a box of porn.

AMENDMENT V

If your Bro finds himself living with a chick, it is no longer acceptable for you to show up uninvited at his door with a box of porn.

AMENDMENT VI

Okay, if a Bro desperately needs to stash his porn somewhere, he *is* allowed to show up uninvited at his Bro's door with a box of porn, *even if* his Bro is living with a chick. Since the Bro's connection with his porn undoubtedly constitutes an older and more meaningful relationship, the box of porn is afforded right of way over the live-in girlfriend, despite the box of porn's inability to get super pissed and withhold sex for the night.

AMENDMENT VII

(Write in your own so that later—when
called upon—you can cite the Bro Code.)

_____

_____

_____

AMENDMENT VIII

A Bro may toss the Bro Code out the window if Scandinavian twins are involved in any capacity.

AMENDMENT IX

A Bro is allowed to play air guitar, provided that the air guitar is made of plastic and connected to a video game system.

AMENDMENT X

A Bro is allowed to publish *The Bro Code* if he stands to make a profit on it.

VIOLATIONS

Violations of the Bro Code may result in a fine of up to $250,000 or in some cases, permanent **dis-Broment**. Unresolved disputes over the Bro Code may be submitted via email to the International Court of Bros at barneystinson@barneysblog.com, provided such disputes include pictures of the chicks involved. But only if they're hot— the chicks, not the disputes.

There is no greater affront to the spirit of the Bro Code than a willing violation. While occasionally a Bro may err due to inebriation, a momentary lapse of judgment, or if a chick is so hot that other Bros would say "he didn't really have a choice," any premeditated infraction of the Bro Code is inexcusable. When a Bro violates the Bro Code, he hurts not only his Bros but also himself, because he is no longer Bro worthy.

It's important to note that there are no tenets of the Bro Code that cannot be discussed in confidence with another Bro, and I would urge a Bro to seek permission from another Bro before doing something, or someone, that he feels might violate this sacred code. Note: A great time to get that permission is when your Bro is super drunk . . . like almost passed out.

If and when a violation occurs, a Bro has the right to administer the offending Bro a level of punishment befitting the infraction. He may choose from the Approved Punishments list.

APPROVED PUNISHMENTS

- Revocation of wingman status
- Text blackout
- Designated all-time tip leaver
- Assigned to solar-refraction seat in living room
- Removal from inappropriate email forwards list
- Waterboarding
- Temporary blacklist from barbecues/football Sundays
- Loss of permanent shotgun status
- Bumped from top position on "not using season tickets" list
- Removal from holiday card mailing list
- Revocation of airport pickup/drop-off privileges
- Must help offended Bro move heavy furniture
- Temporary removal from usual golf foursome
- Must return stuff loaned from offended Bro . . . even stuff he thinks his Bro forgot about
- No longer allowed to borrow the truck
- Offended Bro no longer required to bring beer over

GLOSSARY

Backslide Window—A treacherous window of time following a breakup in which both parties are prone to bone.

Brocassion—An event featuring a bunch of Bros.

Brocedure—A series of events completed by a Bro, but different from the Brolympics.

Bro/Chick Ratio—The gender breakdown at a given venue.

Brocularity—Bro-inspired hijinks.

Broda—(1) A Bro one goes to for wisdom. (2) A really short Bro.

Brode of Silence—Playing dumb or mute when a chick asks about another Bro's history or whereabouts.

Brofession—A Bro job.

Broflation—(1) A sudden increase in female expectations about how dudes should act. (2) A sudden increase in dudes at an event or venue.

Broicide—(1) To kill a Bro. (2) To rack jack a Bro.

Brojo—A Bro's mojo.

Broliferation—Too much use of the word "Bro."

Bronacular—The language of Bros.

Brone—An act of selflessness bestowed upon or by a Bro.

Broner—Excitement over hanging out with Bros e.g., *Ricky popped a broner when his friend rented out the local laser tag arena for his birthday.*

Bro-proofing—Outfitting a space for Bros.

Broshambo—Two dudes playing rock, paper, scissors.

Brotection—When a Bro supplies another Bro with birth control.

Brotorcycle—One of those motorcycles with the sidecar thing.

Bro Train—A convoy of Bros on the move, usually driving to a party

Browling—More than one Bro bowling.

Bro-worker—A Bro at the workplace.

Devil's Threeway—Two dudes, one chick.

Dis-Broment—Removal of "Bro" status.

Dry Spell—A period of any length in which a Bro has not scored.

Jump on the Grenade—The process in which a Bro "takes one for the team" by talking to a hot chick's unattractive friend.

MAC—Memory Assistance and/or Correction.

Quid Pro Bro—Returning a favor by doing a solid for a Bro . . . not that kind of solid.

Rack Jack—To steal a wingman's quarry, often with malicious, premeditated intent.

Tricycle—Two chicks, one dude.

Wingwoman—A female wingman who is also a chick.

SHALLOWEEN ANSWER

	Slutty Cinderella	Slutty Slut	Slutty Ears/Tail	Slutty Nun	9:42 PM	10:56 PM	12:03 AM	2:21 AM	
Viking	X	X	X		X	X		X	9:42 PM
Roosevelt	X		X	X		X	X	X	10:56 PM
Ninja		X	X	X	X		X	X	12:03 AM
Gandhi	X	X		X	X	X	X		2:21 AM
9:42 PM	X		X	X					
10:56 PM		X	X	X					
12:03 AM	X	X	X						
2:21 AM	X	X		X					

THE LEGENDARY SEASON 3

NOW ON DVD

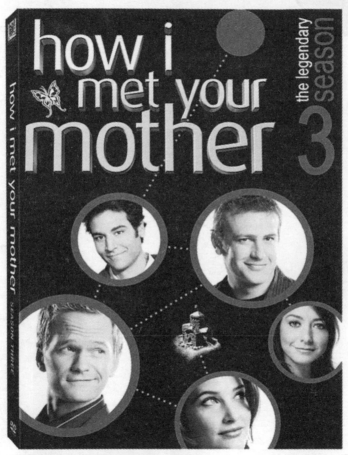

Featuring guest stars
BRITNEY SPEARS,
supermodel **HEIDI KLUM,**
SARAH CHALKE (TV's *Scrubs*)
and **more!**

www.howimetyourmotherdvd.com

© 2008 Twentieth Century Fox Home Entertainment LLC. All Rights Reserved. TWENTIETH CENTURY FOX, FOX
and associated logos are trademarks of Twentieth Century Fox Film Corporation and its related entities.

Seasons 1 & 2 also available